TEAM LEADER'S TOOLKIT

*Ten Tools to Inspire Confidence,
Commitment and Cooperation*

D1551115

TEAM LEADER'S TOOLKIT

*Ten Tools to Inspire Confidence,
Commitment and Cooperation*

Linda Stiles

SkillPath® Publications

Editor: Bill Cowles

Cover design: Jason Sprenger

Layout: Danielle Horn

ISBN: 978-1934-5892-7-4

Printed in the United States of America

Table of Contents

Introduction

Have you ever been on a team that achieved results way beyond expectations because your leader instilled confidence and earned your commitment at every step?

Have you also ever been on a team that never went anywhere or accomplished anything because your leader didn't know where to go or how to get there?

And, have you ever been both of those team leaders?

We've probably all experienced the highs and lows of team leadership at one time or another. Your role as a team leader may not have been an official one, either, because much of leadership occurs from the inside out. A title doesn't always tell the full story.

The purpose of this book is to help you—in whatever role or position of leadership you find yourself—understand the differences between effective and ineffective team leadership and then to master the tools that build confidence, commitment and cooperation in your teams.

PART 1

Personal Skills for Team Leadership

TEAM TOOL #1

Creating a Vision They Will Follow

> "The leader finds the dream and then the people.
> The people find the leader, and then the dream."
>
> – John Maxwell, *The 21 Irrefutable Laws of Leadership*

One of the most overlooked tools to a successful team is the creation of a vision for the team to follow. Not all leaders have the ability to gain or maintain a commitment to a vision. People won't buy into the vision without buying into the leader. A leader's credibility gives the team a reason to follow the vision. The first and most important tool is to create a powerful vision for the team.

There are four questions to ask when creating a team vision:

1. Why do I need a team vision?

2. What do I want team members to do with the vision?

3. How can I create a vision that the team can make their own?

4. Now that I have a vision, what do I do with it?

Mark Towers, in *The ABC's of Empowered Teams*, states that over the last three decades we have grown from a 1:7 supervisor to employee ratio to an average 1:75 ratio. Growth of this magnitude creates a need to rally employees around a common goal of self-motivated productivity.

Why Do I Need a Team Vision?

There are seven reasons why a team vision is such a key to productivity:

1. Visions focus energy
2. Visions direct behavior
3. Visions give purpose to actions
4. Visions support decisions
5. Visions define success
6. Visions create reality
7. Visions provide a rallying cry

Visions Focus Energy

It takes a lot of individual energy to grow within a team. Navigating through the stages of team development (see *Team Tool #2*) requires members to change and adjust their communication. Conflict can arise in the early stages, and having a common goal gives a higher purpose to team member actions. Like a laser, the vision will focus energy away from conflict and onto productivity.

Visions Direct Behavior

A vision can be the deciding factor when individual behavior is not consistent with or in the best interest of the team. When a member's actions have a negative effect on the team's overall productivity, the vision sets the expectations. It defines the rules of business engagement for the team.

Visions Give Purpose to Actions

With a vision, individuals are given a "reason" to behave or produce in a manner that works for the organization. The purpose applies to interactions with team members, project champions, departments, customers or vendors.

Visions Support Decisions

The vision becomes a support system to justify decisions made by the team. It also provides the individual team members a guide for making decisions when a decision is required quickly and without the benefit of team approval.

Visions Define Success

The team must know what success looks like in order to continue performing. A vision defines the destination and validates each step of the process used to get to the destination.

Visions Create Reality

The vision must be stated so that each member can touch, feel and grasp the meaning. Ultimately, a vision must be internalized for the team to perform at its maximum potential. Therefore, the strategic goals of the team or department must be in terms each member can relate to. They must be real.

Visions Provide a Rallying Cry

The personal satisfaction of success creates a sense of euphoria. Having a vision to unite the team makes that euphoria easy to share. The rallying cry will give the team an identity, motivate them and bring cohesion to the group.

With all of these reasons, how can a team get started without a clear, defined and advertised purpose? There are four things that will happen if you do not have a unifying vision:

1. Energy is wasted and momentum is lost

2. Deadlines are missed and the team's credibility is affected

3. Personal agendas become more important than team productivity

4. Team members' focus becomes scattered, and the team leadership is challenged

In *The 360° Leader*, John Maxwell introduces what he calls the "Vision Challenge." A team leader's vision, while it connects to the organization's purpose, must also connect with the team. The challenge for middle managers is to create individual value for a vision the team did not create. The process of team members accepting a vision that someone else created goes something like this:

- The more the leader invests in the vision, the more personally real it will become

- The more real the vision is for the leader, the more team contribution there will be

- The more the team contributes, the more the vision ultimately will belong to the team

To help the team make the vision its own, the team leader must be willing to commit to it. Otherwise, how can the team leader ask the team to follow a rallying cry that he or she is not willing to follow?

What makes a team vision successful? It is:

- Short

- Visible

- Heard often

- An identity

- Related to the organization's vision

- A visual image

- Translated to actions

- Easy to own through team member contribution

A successful vision must inspire internal drive. People are not motivated long-term by only external factors like tangible positive rewards or the avoidance of negative repercussions. While these external controls can move behavior to the required result, the ultimate objective of a successful vision is sustainability. When a team member is working toward an internalized purpose, they will continue to perform whether the external rewards are given or not.

The GE organizational vision is "We bring good things to life." If you were charged with creating a vision for your Customer Service Department within GE, you might choose "We are a good thing in the life of our customers." It is short, easy to identify with and can directly relate to the actions needed to create the "good" customer experience. Also notice how it relates to the main corporate vision. No matter what division, what the customer call is about or if the team is responsible for implementing a business project—everything they do is focused on being a "good thing" in the life of their customers.

What Do I Want Team Members to Do With the Vision?

There are four levels of vision acceptance your team members may display:

1. Some will never see the vision. These team members will be sporadic performers, responding only to the external controls that appeal to them.

2. Others will see the vision but not pursue it. These members are followers and will perform as long as you, the leader, direct them.

3. Then there are people who can see the vision clearly and will pursue it. These are your team achievers. They have accepted the vision as their own and use it to direct and fulfill their purpose.

4. Finally, some team members not only will see the vision and pursue it, but will help others make the vision their own. These individuals have set themselves apart as the next generation of leaders in your organization and are the keys to your succession plan.

Focused purpose does more than just link the team to the organization's business goals. It is also meant to bring time efficiency to the team members. When musicians of the Houston Symphony Orchestra were asked what they most admired about their conductor, they responded "He does not waste our time." This is a testament to the individual benefit the conductor's focused purpose brought to his team. The conductor was known for his commitment to the vision of his organization and he seldom took time away from his team for public interviews.

How Do I Create a Vision That the Team Can Make Their Own?

There are four steps to defining vision for the team:

Step #1—Know your organization's vision. This vision is usually set by the organization's leadership and represents why and how the business exists. The team must contribute to this vision or it will be difficult to justify the team's existence. If the organization's vision is not known, look to these sources:

- Company Web site

- HR Department

- Company president (or the Executive Assistant)

Step #2—What does or will the team do? List the business tasks and who will be responsible. Think in terms of the services provided to the rest of the company or to customers.

Step #3—What value does or will the team's work bring to the organization's vision? List the result of the team's tasks that were defined in Step #2. How do these results contribute to the organization?

Step #4—Create a short statement that represents the team's value to the organization's vision. This will be the primary vision statement. Use the same words that are used in the organization's value statement. It should be no more than one sentence—the shorter, the better. State the vision so that it can clearly point to actions that will produce desired results. If the vision can be translated into actions, the members have a better chance of contributing to the vision and making it their own.

Let's go through the steps and create a strong team vision statement.

Step #1—Write your organization's vision.

_____

_____

_____

Step #2—Define your team, department or project tasks and responsibilities.

_____

_____

_____

Step #3—How does the responsibility of your team link to the organizational vision statement?

_____

_____

_____

Step #4—What phrases represent your team's contribution in terms of the organization's value statement? Use these to create a short, direct vision statement.

_____

_____

_____

With a clear direction, the tools to get the job done and your trust, you have boldly empowered your team to achieve success.

Now That I Have a Vision, What Do I Do With It?

Just because a team vision has been created, don't expect members to automatically make it the driving force behind their work. It will take some time, and it is a leader's responsibility to keep them focused on the unifying purpose. The leader must surround and immerse the members with the vision so it becomes a rallying cry for action. Team members should see and hear it often.

Consider putting the vision on:

- Wall hangings
- Laminated pages around the coffee pot
- Framed pages for office or meeting spaces
- Computer-generated banners
- Promotional pens or pencils
- Sticky notes
- Headers for office forms
- T-shirts
- Coffee mugs
- E-mail signatures
- Computer screen savers

The true test of "stick-ability" is not whether the team verbally commits to the team vision, but rather, do they take action on it? Every position on the team should be related to the vision. People get very excited when they see themselves in the vision.

Relate each project or assignment to the team vision. This means the team vision should transcend a particular project and be applicable to the team's business purpose. Some teams are formed for a specific strategic reason, in which case, the vision will change once the team is adjourned. (See *Team Tool #2 – Navigating the Stages of Team Development* to find out more about revising a team vision.)

Each team success should be communicated as it relates to the vision. Communication should be varied, but at least one consistent and dependable channel must exist.

Let's say a consistent channel of communication to all team members, management and other interested departments is a weekly e-mail. Always send the e-mail on the same day and target the same time on that day. Maintain a consistent but efficient structure. Create a Top Five report that gives the top five accomplishments of the week or month. Each item should be quantified. Put all accomplishments in measurable terms.

Here are a few things to measure:

- Project time

- Tasks

- Milestones in assignments

- Cost savings

- Time spent or saved

- Productivity increase

- Performance improvement

Here are a few recognizable terms of measurement:

- Percentage

- Number

- Dollars

- Hours

- Manpower

- Units

Quantifiable results ultimately will prove the success of the team as well as the leader's skills.

Communication of the team's success will create an after-effect that may not be expected:

- It will differentiate the team members as top performers. Because of these skills, they may be recruited by other managers or departments within the organization. They may be offered opportunities with other companies. The leader's challenge has been to build each team member. They will choose to continue to grow with a dynamic team or expand their skills in another organization.

- The best and the brightest employees within the company will be drawn to this dynamic team opportunity. High productivity of a team creates value for its members. Value creates pride and pride is contagious. Being on such a dynamic team will become the envy of the organization.

A solid vision will support a team and give it purpose. But bottom-line productivity must come from the performance of each member. A team leader's challenge is to guide the members through the individual adjustments needed to become the best performers they can be.

TEAM TOOL #2

Navigating the Stages of Team Development

> "If you could get all of the people in an organization rowing in the same direction, you could dominate any industry, in any market, against any competition, at any time."
>
> – Patrick Lencioni, *The Five Dysfunctions of a Team*

Every team goes through phases in establishing productive relationships. Just as with any relationship, a team must set a foundation of respect and trust in order to work effectively together. This foundation will be the key to team success and organizational profitability.

In a perfect world, co-workers get together, learn how to work with each other, take on assignments and efficiently complete their projects. In the real world, semi-functional co-workers get together, struggle to understand each other, have difficulty agreeing on how to approach assignments and encounter many obstacles while trying to achieve their goals. Individual skills and personal perceptions affect intra-team relationships and determine the levels of performance that can be expected.

Teams are fluid. They ebb and flow with the tides of emotions and perceptions. Do any of the following observations of team interaction sound familiar?

- John thinks he is the leader. He "barks" his requests to other team members.

- Sarah talks too much and wastes her time as well as the time of others

- Susan can't stand the conflict so she has left the team for a new position in the customer service department

- Brad does not agree with the team decisions but is not comfortable speaking up

These behavioral issues can pop up or move into the teambuilding process at any point. New members come into existing teams, successful individuals accept other opportunities. The stages of team development create a matrix depending on which stage each team member might be in at any one time. Knowing what stage team members are passing through will help the team leader to take each working relationship to its highest performance level.

There are several published team process models. The most popular is the five-stage model of team development. We will use this model as a foundation but will overlay a three-level performance driver model to help the team leader navigate between the stages. Team members will move through the five stages at different times and at different paces. The team leader should recognize the stages and have the techniques to make it a smooth ride to productivity for each member.

In *Organizational Behavior: Concepts, Controversies and Applications,* Stephen Robbins identifies the patterns of intra-team relational development as a five-stage model:

1. Forming

2. Storming

3. Norming

4. Performing

5. Adjourning

The Forming Stage

As the team is established or as a new person moves into an existing team, first impressions will lay the foundation for the working relationship. If the foundation is based on mutual respect, the working relationship will become a productive one. If the foundation is based on any of the following personal mindsets, the team relationships are destined for problems.

- What can I do to impress my team?

- What can I do to be accepted by my team?

- What can this team do for me and my career?

During the forming stage, perceptions play a major role in judging other team members. Sometimes a wrong determination is made too quickly. When there is a gap between our assessment and reality, conflict begins. This is what fuels the team moving into the storming stage.

Team member energy during the forming stage is focused on the individual. There is usually a feeling of uncertainty about purpose. The team leader's vision will help create purpose during this stage. (See *Team Tool #1* to discover how to create a vision for the team.) At the end, each team member must feel that they are part of an established group.

The Storming Stage

When conflict occurs within a productive working relationship, then conflict is good. During this stage the members are learning how to work with each other. It's important for the team to recognize the value each member brings to the table and give each member credit for it, and sometimes that realization travels through conflict.

Conflict within the team comes from the three "Mis-es":

- **Mis-understandings**—the product of poor listening

- **Mis-conceptions**—the product of poor assumptions

- **Mis-information**—the product of poor clarification

If the forming stage did not establish a foundation of mutual respect, the three "Mis-es" surely will show up. To overcome the effect of the three "Mis-es," put these three skills into action:

Skill #1: Avoid Misunderstandings

Be a good listener. The foundation of trust and respect is listening.

- Maintain good eye contact. Stay focused on the team member.

- Do not interrupt. Let the other person finish their sentences.

- Recap or acknowledge what you hear

Skill #2: Escape Misconceptions

Be aware of your window of perception. Our window to the world is etched by our life experiences and can create problems.

- Judgments

- Biases

- Opinions

Skill #3: Shake Off Misinformation

Know when and how to clarify.

- When possible, recap in writing

- Follow your gut—it is part experience

The energy of the storming stage is focused on problem-solving. At the end, there should be an established leader, and rules of engagement should begin to take form. These rules can be formalized in a team charter. (See *Team Tool #4* on how to lay a solid foundation for team expectations.)

The Norming Stage

The relationship between team members now begins to settle down. The members focus on cohesion and begin to learn how to best use each other's skills. This also is the first point where the team charter (defined and discussed in more detail on page 64) is enforced. Repercussions are understood. Members are held accountable. Accommodations are made for the different communication and behavioral styles of the members in the spirit of cooperation.

Following are two possible scenarios that might be seen during this stage:

- Bob was pushing the team members to complete tasks before the deadlines while in the storming stage. Tempers flared and team members took his demanding statements personally. As the relationships moved into the norming stage, team members realized Bob's main focus was to get the project completed, and members learned to clarify the agreed-upon deadlines without losing their tempers.

- Patsy was always late with her assignments and to team meetings. In the storming stage, this created conflict with those who depended on her tasks. By the norming stage, expectations were established with repercussions for noncompliance, and Patsy was held accountable for her actions.

Working through the norming stage requires member acceptance and a willingness to build productive business relationships. Using the team charter will reduce the emotional influence and emphasize a business foundation for the team. The energy in this phase is focused on work balance. By the end, the group will have a structure and each member will have a set of established expectations of their role. This will move the team into the most productive stage of team process.

The Performing Stage

Wouldn't it be great if all the team relationships were as productive, predictable and positive as they are in this stage? Established teams reach and maintain this high level of performance through the constant motivation of completion. Assimilation of new members goes quickly, and established team relationships serve as a model for behavior.

Productive team relationships can be applied to many different projects, goals or programs. In other words, it is no longer about the expertise but about the expectation of performance within the team.

The energy of this stage focuses on task completion. Members trust and depend on each other. This is the last stage of development for permanent teams like organizational departments. For temporary teams, the next stage provides a stepping stone for the team members and the organization if managed well.

The Adjourning Stage

In today's workplace, most teams are established for a purpose and usually do not disband unless there are organizational changes. This stage could include some of the following duties:

- Finalization of documentation

- Transference of skills to department staff from subject matter experts

- Transference of responsibility to outsourced entities

Team members are recognized for their contributions and then assigned to another project. Successful team experiences can provide an organization with some sustaining skills:

- Process knowledge

- Team charter experience

- Consistent performance results

The energy of this stage focuses on the maintenance and retention of the team result. At the end, there should be a complete handover, shutdown or transference of the team purpose.

Throughout the five-stage model, there are three levels of performance drivers. These are the personal motivators behind team members' actions. They have been identified as:

- **Self-focused**—actions benefit self

- **Team-focused**—actions benefit another member of the team or the team itself

- **Vision-focused**—actions benefit the team purpose

During the initial stages of team development, members have not made a link to other members for task support, so they are more dependent on themselves for team contribution. They are self-focused. As team members move through conflict and establish ground rules, they begin to use each other to be productive. They become team-focused. Ultimately, individual motivation for action becomes to produce for and get gratification from the team vision. At this point, the vision has been internalized.

The following table shows the relation between the stages of team development and the performance drivers. The description of how to recognize the stage a member is in may help with the activity following the table.

Team Member Stages	Performance Drivers	Purpose of the Stage	How to Recognize	How to Transition From This Stage
Forming	Self	Open relationships	Members are welcoming	Mutual respect and trust, finding common ground
Storming	Self to Team	Set relationship boundaries and team expectations	Members are challenging	Set expectations, deal with conflict, create a team charter
Norming	Team	Bring the team together as work group	Members are accommodating	Lean on each member's strongest skill
Performing	Team to Vision	Focus on productivity	Members are connecting	Recognize members and preserve knowledge
Adjourning	Vision to Self	Document and hand off	Members are completing	

List your team members' names at the top of each column and again in the left-hand column. At the intersection of each set of names, write which stage you think that relationship is in according to the five stages of team development.

Members' Names → ↓					

Which team member relationships need help moving to the next stages?

_____

_____

_____

_____

List two things you can do to help each team member transition to a productive stage:

Member_____   1._____

                                                         2._____

Member_____   1._____

                                                          2._____

Member_____   1._____

                                                          2._____

Member_____   1._____

                                                          2._____

Member_____   1._____

                                                          2._____

Member_____   1._____

                                                          2._____

> "Start doing what is necessary, then do what is possible,
> and suddenly you are doing the impossible."
>
> – St. Francis of Assisi

A team leader's position can be a difficult one if some of the basic personal leadership skills are not in place. There are three critical skills that leaders need to understand and practice so they can use them strategically.

1. When and how to give easy and sincere praise

2. When and how to deliver criticism that is constructive, corrective and concern-based

3. When and how to establish a self-preservation system that will support leader growth

In a poll taken of Chamber of Commerce members across the United States, the number one thing that the respondents thought employers could do to motivate their workers had nothing to do with money. They simply wanted to feel that they were appreciated and receive praise for a job well done. A Gallup Organization poll was taken of 2,000 workers, and 69% responded that they valued praise and appreciation more than money. The same research showed that four out of five respondents were motivated to do a better job when they received specific and sincere praise.

When and How to Give Easy and Sincere Praise

To build and retain team members, praise must come easily for the team leader. It all starts with expecting the best from the team and trusting them to perform. With a positive, expectant attitude, the leader will be more aware of the positive behavior. Our feedback to team members tends toward correction and not celebration.

Positive feedback will build relationships for 360° around you. Praising your staff builds their confidence and motivates them. Praising your peers creates allies and builds a support system for those difficult times when you need someone to confide in. Praising your manager should be seen as support and not unconditional agreement, which may be perceived as insincere and could have negative consequences.

Catching your staff and those around you doing something "right" sets the tone for working relationships within your team. In the book *Whale Done!*, Ken Blanchard and his co-authors translate the positive training techniques used at Sea World and apply them to the workplace. One of the techniques used at Sea World is to pair a new wild whale with a seasoned trained whale. The "training whale" leads by example and sets the learning model for the new whale. In the workplace, the team leader is the "training whale" and will set the tone of the team by positively reinforcing correct behavior.

According to *The Measure of a Leader* by Aubrey and James Daniels, there are five key factors about positive reinforcement. Positive feedback is:

- **Highly personal.** Praise does not come "one-size-fits-all." Know your staff and what works for each individual.

- **Earned.** Praising just to be nice will support the wrong behavior and dilute the value of all positive feedback given.

- **Frequent.** Positive feedback must still be specific and sincere. Frequent enough to have an impact but not enough to lose its value.

- **Immediate.** As team leaders, to have an impact on behavior we must take the same approach as we do when raising kids and training puppies. Feedback needs to be immediate for them to relate it to the behavior.

- **Best if it is not financial.** This form of positive reinforcement loses it impact over time.

To give your praise more value, the following are eight tips to "kick it up a notch." It is important to be:

1. **Specific:** "Good job" is not as valuable as "Good job on that report"

2. **Sincere:** They can hear it in the tone of your voice

3. **Timely:** Praise immediately for maximum impact

4. **Personal:** Use their name

5. **Positive:** Don't take the back door approach with "Well, at least you didn't mess it up this time"

6. **Public:** Recognize a team member's accomplishments in front of their peers or recognize your colleagues to a third party

7. **Proactive:** Tell them what value the continued behavior will have for them

8. **Physical:** Use nonverbal support actions—thumbs-up, handshake, etc.

Praise is not typically thought of as a behavioral modification tool, but it is very effective in turning around nonproductive behavior. *Whale Done!* emphasizes the importance of using praise to support any positive behavior change. The more attention you pay to a behavior, the more you will get of it, so why not give positive feedback for positive change of negative behavior? During the discipline process, we take the punitive approach and wait to punish instead of praising positive change. It is human nature to wait until they fail before giving them feedback, which pays attention to the behavior we do not want. To implement a positive reinforcement plan during the discipline process, meet once a week for 10 minutes to force yourself to recognize the person for improving their behavior.

There is a negative side to positive feedback which you should be aware of. Watch out for unintentional positive feedback and the message it sends. The natural tendency is to give reduced workload to a poor performer or to pay overtime to a slow worker. We don't realize that our behavior is sending a message of approval and support for behavior that we do not want. (See more information about this in *Team Tool #5 – Productively Managing Team Conflict.*)

If positive feedback is too frequent and not tied to an accomplishment, workers will begin to expect it. Two examples might be:

- Bringing doughnuts to work on Friday

- Having a pizza lunch once a month

These popular treats may have started out as a reward but became expected—almost a tradition—when the team no longer connected the reward with an achievement.

Conversely, if praise is withheld, any positive change that has been made will become extinct due to lack of appreciation. The message that the behavior is not valued is being sent.

Remember, the more attention you pay to a behavior, the more you get of it, so pay attention to the behavior you want to continue.

The team leader does not always have to deliver the praise personally. If the work environment has a process in place to support positive behavior efforts through a peer recognition program, then positive support can come from others and be just as meaningful. Positive reinforcement can come in many forms, but praise is the easiest, cheapest and most personal way to improve performance, and knowing how to deliver it is very important.

When and How to Deliver Criticism That Is Constructive, Corrective and Concern-based

We all like to be positive, but there are times when the team leader must address negative behavior or nonproductive performance. Knowing how to effectively deliver constructive criticism is a must-have tool in every leader's toolkit.

First, let's take a look at some situations warranting constructive criticism:

- Nonproductive performance

- Negative behavior

- Bad attitude

- Team-destructive communication

What are some of the excuses we use to not confront a team member about their behavior?

Confidence Issues	Perception Issues
Fear of conflict	They won't like me
I don't know how	They won't change
I don't feel comfortable correcting them	They are my friend
I am tired of dealing with this person	I can't handle the conflict

These excuses are broken down into two areas. Confidence issues take knowledge and practice to eliminate. Perception issues will require that you look at all problems with an unemotional eye. Team problems are productivity problems, and your responsibility as a team leader is to manage productivity. You have the ability to remove all of these excuses through awareness and personal growth. In *Personal Tool #2* (page 49), you will learn to make the personal change you will need to effectively confront team problems.

There are three levels of constructive criticism. If your team reports directly to you, then all three of these options are available to you. If your team is a cross-functional one where you're not directly responsible for evaluations of your team members, then their direct manager should be aware that you are addressing an issue and should be involved in or deliver the second and third levels of correction.

1. As soon as you observe a behavior or discover a productivity problem, the team member needs to be made aware of the problem. The first touch point with the team member would be an ***awareness meeting***. The productivity issue needs to be presented, supported and discussed. Your attitude should be one of concern for their productivity or outside influences that could affect their performance. Avoid the punitive approach. Taking a punishment attitude will affect any trust or respect you may have established with the team member.

2. If the behavior continues, the next touch point is a ***corrective session***. This would involve coaching or a performance improvement plan for the team member. Remember to include any other direct management if this team member does not report directly to you. Your attitude here should focus on specific corrective steps and defined accountability measures. If correction is not made, then your concern is that the next step may jeopardize the power of your team.

3. The final touch point is the ***discipline steps***. These will be defined in your organization's handbook and are serious. At this point, there is a risk of losing some knowledge and some productivity. The problems being addressed may have a negative effect on the team's productivity, but understand that whatever work the problem member is doing will have to be assigned to another team member and that could create a balance and prioritization problem.

If issues are not addressed immediately, three things will happen:

1. The behavior will continue. The team member has not been told to stop or change the behavior.

2. Others will start behaving the same way. They think the behavior is acceptable.

3. The leader's credibility is negatively affected. Peers and management know that you are not supporting the policies.

The right words will not just pop out of your mouth. Plan what you will say, practice it and deliver it with confidence. Two suggestions seem consistent with most management teaching when it comes to constructive criticism structure:

1. For awareness meetings or to start a corrective conversation, start with a support statement. Make it specific, and it has to be true. "I appreciate your good work" is not specific enough to show confidence that the team member can improve. "I appreciate the thorough approach you took when you put the report together yesterday" goes straight to the point. After the statement of support, move into the behavioral issue at hand. Stay focused on no more than two issues at a time.

2. State the issue from your perspective. Use "I" statements to inform them about what you as the team leader have seen, understood, discovered, etc. The point is to stay away from using the accusatory "you" to avoid fueling a confrontation.

Criticism is often the dreaded part of team leadership. Take the approach that anything constructive is the direct opposite of destructive, so behavioral or performance issues should be discussed immediately and from a point of concern, not punishment.

Establishing a Self-preservation System That Will Support Leader Growth

As new team leaders, we focus on the external challenges of our position and neglect our personal, internal challenges. If we do not develop the team leader mindset, our performance, our productivity and, ultimately, our health can be affected.

Following are seven "Personal Tools" to put in your toolbox. Building these skills will help you successfully lead others through the same path of personal growth.

Personal Tool #1 – Leader, Lead Thyself

The team is constantly watching to see how the leader will handle critical workplace basics. Check the following personal habits that you manage well:

- ☐ I keep my emotions in check
- ☐ I manage my time
- ☐ I can set realistic priorities
- ☐ I channel my energy productively
- ☐ I control my assumptions, perceptions and opinions
- ☐ I watch my words
- ☐ I have a healthy work/life balance

If these personal habits are difficult for the team leader, you can understand the challenge the team might have in putting them in place. Pick the most challenging habit and reach for the next tool.

Personal Tool #2 – Leader, Change Thyself

If any of the habits in Personal Tool #1 are recognized as a problem, then the team leader has just taken the first step in the six steps to change. Climb up this staircase to successful change so you can in turn help your team make changes.

To define each step of the change process:

1. **Awareness:** Something is not working

2. **Desire:** There is pressure, you are overwhelmed, and these emotions drive you to take action

3. **Knowledge:** Find out what is needed and take control to change the behavior

4. **Practice:** Take action; if you do not, things will never change

5. **Success:** Begin to experience the euphoria of productive change

6. **Habit:** Experience the long-term benefits of your efforts

This model is presented in the Employee Development Systems, Inc. program "Increasing Personal Effectiveness" and is the key to personal success. Your team will model what they see, so be the "Training Whale"—not only in your work habits but also in personal growth.

Remember, effective change always begins within.

Personal Tool #3 – Leader, Lighten Up

There was a time when fun in the workplace was considered nonproductive. In today's workplace, nonproduction is characterized by high stress levels, increased sick time, constant connection through technology and increased competition. Every opportunity for a stress break contributes to a more productive team when they are intensely focused on your team vision.

Dr. William Frey of Stanford University advises we should laugh at least 15 times a day. Laughing is called "internal jogging." It reduces stress, increases creativity, raises enthusiasm, improves productivity and keeps team members around longer.

Take 15 Laugh Laps around that virtual, mental track. Along the way, share them with your team.

Personal Tool #4 – Leader, Let Go

Two emotional areas of management plague us when we become team leaders. The first, the traditional perception that decision making is the sole responsibility of the manager, can rob your team of a high-octane fuel that could supercharge their performance. The decision-making process within a well-oiled team should fire on three cylinders:

1. The team vision sets the focus of any decisions (*Team Tool #1*)

2. The team charter determines how decisions will be made (*Team Tool #4*)

3. Leadership support

Set aside all ego issues and empower the team by teaching them and supporting their decision-making process.

The second emotional challenge is that we are responsible for giving credit to the team, but often it is not the practice of our management to recognize leadership abilities and give credit to us. Consider starting a monthly Top Five Report to your management. List your top five team achievements, give the team credit and quantify their results. Chances are, your manager will use those reports to support your annual performance review. This will make the credit you ultimately get both solid and public. Most of all, get rid of that nagging voice saying that no one appreciates your work.

TEAM TOOL #4

Laying the Foundation for a Productive Team

"People naturally follow leaders stronger than themselves."

– John Maxwell, *The 21 Irrefutable Laws of Leadership*

As the team leader, we want to make sure that the team has the greatest opportunity for success. It is our responsibility to lay a solid foundation for performance, team expectations, productivity and acceptable behavior. *Team Tool #2 – Navigating the Stages of Team Development* defines the process that the team will go through to build high-performance relationships. A team will be fluid, with members moving in and out, so no two relationships are at the same level. This chapter will present the personal and process standards that will become the team expectations for working together.

There are three characteristics that are important for team members to have in their relationships: trust, credibility and respect. The four key points we will discuss are:

1. Why these are important

2. What it looks like when team members have these characteristics

3. How you can foster this in their relationships

4. What happens when there is no trust, credibility or respect

Why Are Trust, Credibility and Respect Important?

Of the three founding characteristics of a powerful team—trust, respect and credibility—trust is the most important. If the team trusts the team leader, they will trust the message that is given and take action on it. If the team members trust each other, they will share thoughts and needs without fear of criticism or degradation. Trust also can be a significant factor in whether or not an individual is satisfied with their organization or their team. Without building trust, the leader cannot lead, and team members will not function at their peak performance level. The important thing about trust is that it must be given in order to be gained.

Once trust is established, the opportunity to gain the other person's respect has been earned. Some team leaders or members try to demand respect because of position, knowledge, seniority, credentials, experience or whatever they perceive is of great importance. Placing a greater impression of ourselves over the perceptions of others implies that we have no trust in that person's judgment, and respect cannot follow. If trust is open collaboration and respect is honoring accomplishments, then credibility is the track record of commitments. Follow-through can establish or destroy credibility. If trust is violated, confidence is lost. Without confidence, respect will be questioned and credibility will be affected.

What Does a Team With Trust in and Respect for Each Other Look Like?

What will it look like when your team has put the foundation of trust in place? Productive collaboration will be at the heart of everything the team will do. The team members will be comfortable with sharing their weaknesses, their skill deficiencies and their mistakes or with joking about some of their interpersonal shortcomings. These vulnerabilities are easy to share when surrounded by a support system. Time and energy are efficiently used in task and behavior management. Meetings are efficient because asking and giving help does not involve emotional barriers. Team members will act on the information they receive from the team because the source can be trusted. The credibility of the team will bring a strong sense of attachment and give each member a greater sense of ownership in what the team stands for.

Mistakes and problems are discussed to the benefit of the team. No emotions! No egos! At this point, the primary benefit of trust is to accelerate learning. Making each part function better will transform the whole into a high-performance machine.

How Can You Build Trust as the Solid Foundation for a Team?

First, trust must be given in order to be received. Trust has been defined as open collaboration. In order to collaborate, we must first open our ears. Listening is the source of trust. Listening will help you discover what is important to someone so that you can support that need or become openly collaborative.

Harry Cleberg, CEO of Farmland Industries, which was the largest farmer-owned cooperative in North America at one time, would spend 200 days a year traveling to talk to employees and cooperative members. He would hold small group sessions called "listening posts" to gather information, concerns and accolades about the company's progress. His attitude and his action earned the trust of his employees. He was visible and approachable, and employees returned that trust to him and the business. He created open collaboration.

Listening is very simple. It only has three steps and they are easy to visualize:

1. Erase the whiteboard of your mind and stand with marker in hand, ready to take notes

2. Look directly at the speaker sitting in the front row of your mind

3. After you have written a few things on your whiteboard, confirm them

If the whiteboard has been erased when you start, there will be no distractions and there will be no biases. There should be no interruptions unless it applies to what you have written on the whiteboard.

By practicing good listening skills, a proactive leader continues to set the tone for the team, to lay the foundation and to lead by example. Leaders will trust the team members' words, thus demonstrating respect for them. Knowing what is important to someone shows you more precisely how to reinforce and motivate them.

To draw the team closer together, it is best to occasionally get the members out of the workplace. Different work environments, schedules, policies or shifts would dictate what would be appropriate for your group. Here are some suggestions:

- Lunch or dinner out of the office

- An afternoon bowling game

- A long lunch at the movies

- A car wash in the parking lot

- Lunch at the park

If getting the team out of the office is a challenge, gather them in the conference room for some time off together. Brainstorm with the team to come up with some ideas of things they would like to do.

In addition to getting to know each other outside of work, learning something unique about each other will help to build a bridge of friendship. Here is an exercise that will help get those relationships started.

Secret Identity:

- Give each person a 3x5 card—all of the cards should be the same color
- Have everyone write down something on their card that no one would know about them (but they don't mind sharing)
- Collect, shuffle and redistribute the cards in random order
- Each person writes on the card the name of whom they think the card describes
- After about 15 minutes, collect the cards
- Read each description and have the correct person stand up

This exercise establishes uniqueness for the team members.

Team Effectiveness Exercise:

- On a piece of paper, list each of the team members (including the team leader) down the left-hand side
- Make two columns on the right side of the page
- In one column, write one positive contribution for each member
- Facilitate a discussion about each member's strength and in the second column note how each contribution can make the team work
- Ask the others how to utilize these individual strengths within the team

When There Is No Trust in the Team, What Will Happen?

If basic personal standards are not put in place, all of the necessary relationships within the team are affected. Between the team leader and team member, actions are not completed, instructions are ignored, problems reoccur and the cost of team performance increases.

The most damaging manifestation of leader/member mistrust is micromanagement on the part of the team leader. Micromanagement is defined as continual unsolicited updates on work beyond agreed-upon deadlines. This becomes more of an ego-support practice than a leadership practice and becomes more competitive than supportive.

Losing trust within the team increases competition and information guarding. This will lead to wasted time and energy managing their behavior and interactions. Team members act on personal agendas rather than team solutions, so problems and issues are never resolved in a reproducible manner. Team members may dread or avoid meetings and not ask for or give help to others.

Failure to follow through also will result in loss of trust. Follow-through is a measure of credibility. If the leader has a low level of credibility, the members will possibly produce only if they are being watched. The members need money to be motivated, are not supportive of the organization, feel unappreciated and are probably looking for another job.

The team will look to the team leader to see the model for relationships. The best way to lay the foundation of trust, respect and credibility is to model that behavior. Be Ken Blanchard's model of the "Training Whale."

Putting a process foundation in place for the team gives it structure. There are two parts to the structure a team needs:

1. **Ground rules for team interaction.** A Team Charter will be created to set team interaction ground rules.

2. **Well-managed meetings.** Rules of Engagement for Meetings will be established to productively manage team meetings.

We will approach learning about this structure in three steps:

1. What is meant by process foundation and structure for the team?

2. Why do I need a process foundation?

3. How can I put these tools in place for my team?

What Is a Process Foundation?

The use of teams in the workplace has increased dramatically since the Baby Boomer generation forced organizations to use teams as a way to involve more people in the decision-making process. This was for both strategic protection of the organization as well as employee satisfaction. In the book *Tools for Teams: Building Effective Teams in the Workplace*, the process foundation sets the business standards that are expected of the team. Standards such as how decisions will be made, how conflict will be handled, acceptable behavior for meetings and the consequences for not following the standards are all part of the process foundation.

Why Is a Process Foundation Needed?

Tools for Teams techniques have worked successfully in the academic and professional world. The premise of putting a process around managing team interactions is to create a fair and consistent model that can be followed no matter how long you have been in the team. Newcomers and old-timers alike will follow the same process for decision making, conflict resolution, etc. The standards provide a recognizable, dependable model to efficiently incorporate or disseminate team members. The final concern is to keep the productivity up through times of challenge.

How Can These Tools Be Put in Place?

Every team member will need to be involved in creating, using or updating any of the structure tools that the team puts in place. Two tools used as control mechanisms for the team are:

- The Team Charter
- Rules of Engagement for Meetings

A Team Charter is to be viewed just like a beginning "charter" for any group or organization. A charter defines purpose, team members, skills, the decision process, possible support resources, responsibility and accountability boundaries, conflict management and consequences. Following are the section guidelines for building an effective charter that will support the productivity of the team:

- **Purpose:** The purpose of the team is usually defined by the team vision. The type of team should also be defined here. Types may include temporary, permanent, cross-functional, departmental, project-specific, etc.

- **Team members:** Each of the team members, including the team leader, are listed here. Include titles (team title or purpose within the team), contact information and preference and emergency information with conditions.

- **Skills:** Business and personal skills of each team member are listed. This list can be used as a support reference for the other team members. The list could include the member's challenge area with an understanding and discussion of which team member could support that challenge area. This section can be done in conjunction with the Team Efficiency exercise listed earlier in this chapter that focused on members' strengths.

- **Responsibility boundaries:** In this section you will set the expectations of team member behavior. It is the team member's responsibility to follow these standards. If nonconformance becomes a problem, consequences will be delivered through the conflict resolution process. Here is a sampling of issues that could be discussed, addressed and established before a conflict would arise:

  — *Contribution:* This is your expectation of participation in tasks, discussions and scheduling

  — *Deadlines:* List the expectation of performance against deadlines and the process for informing the team of potential deadline risk

  — *Communication:* Define allowable meeting options (teleconference, video conference, call-in, substitutes), determine the standard of communication to keep everyone informed and determine if there will be a regular group meeting (when, where, how)

  — *Decision making:* Collectively determine how the team will make decisions. Some examples would be democratic, multi-level approval, leader driven and autocratic.

  — *Consequences:* This is a list of what happens within the team if someone does not meet the documented expectations listed in the Team Charter

There should be multiple levels of consequences, depending on the impact of the infraction, that should be thoroughly addressed.

For a first offense, an annoying "junk task" or assignment to a mundane task, or cleaning the coffee pot for a week or buying the team a round of soft drinks might be an appropriate consequence. For an issue that impacts the team goal, assignment of the task to someone else for completion, or reassignment of the team member to a less critical area, removal of name from specific task or additional training could be given.

Define several levels of infractions so the consequences can match the level of influence the nonproductive behavior has. Here are some examples:

Level 1 – Annoyance Level	Annoyance task
Level 2 – Productivity disturbance	Group fix, group reassignment
Level 3 – Productivity impact	Reassignment of task
Level 4 – Productivity interruption	Possible release from team

- **Conflict resolution process:** There are three corrective bodies within a team environment: the individual, the group and the team leader. When the team defines a resolution process, it should stop once an issue is handed to the team leader. The leader is responsible for managing performance issues through the organization's disciplinary action program. Here are a few guidelines that could be considered as steps in the team conflict resolution process:

  — Have a 24-hour rule. Discuss any concerns or clarify any misunderstandings within 24 hours.

  — Discuss issues in person—face-to-face, or over the phone. Avoid e-mail when initially introducing a problem. There is too much room for incorrect perceptive interpretation.

  — Present problems with "I" statements

  — If the issue continues, include the team leader in the next discussion of the problem

  — If the issue continues, it should be handed over to the team leader for further attention

- **Support resources:** List the people within the company who have a stake in the outcome of the team. This could include champions, executives, subject matter experts, system users, vendors, customers, consultants etc. Resources also could include purchased support systems, material, reference manuals or other physical knowledge sources.

Putting a charter together may seem tedious, but it is necessary to define the rules for team interaction. These rules will be the key to easily transferring new members into the team while maintaining the flow of productivity.

Team meetings can drain productivity if not handled well. One major corporation determined that it spent from 7% to 15% of its personnel budget on meetings. Other sources have reported that 50% of the time spent in meetings is unproductive and 25% of meeting time is spent addressing totally irrelevant issues. The second process foundation tool to maintain team performance is the Rules of Engagement for Meetings. This form steps team members through planning, documenting and following up on meetings. It uses the "4P" approach to meeting planning: **Purpose, People, Plan** and **Process.**

1. **Purpose:** What is this meeting for? Information? Decision making? Group communication?

2. **People:** List key players, additional people needed for decisions and those that need to be kept informed. Not all need to be present but may need to get meeting notes.

3. **Plan:** This is the agenda. List items, persons responsible and the time allotted.

4. **Process:** This includes the meeting results. Who was assigned what? What decisions were made? What was discussed? Key points?

On the Rules of Engagement for Meetings, two extra P's have been added:

5. **Parking lot:** A collection of associated ideas that need to be researched, discussed next time or tabled but not forgotten. This can be used to take notes on issues or questions that would get the meeting off track.

6. **P's and Q's:** Proper meeting behavior is defined for participants to understand the Rules of Engagement. Examples include: Keep an open mind. No cheap shots. Participate. Clarify. Give everyone a chance to speak. Stay focused on project issues and not emotional issues. No rehashing of past resolved issues. Abide by group decisions. Maintain confidentiality. Be polite. No defensiveness.

Add those items that are particular to the organizational culture that can become a problem in meetings. The advantage is to have them discussed ahead of the problem moment.

While the Rules of Engagement for Meetings helps in planning meetings, here is a checklist of good personal habits to maximize what attendees get from a meeting.

- ☐ Qualify attendance (Am I the best person for this meeting?)
- ☐ Prepare for the meeting
- ☐ Be on time
- ☐ Clarify information when needed
- ☐ Be precise—speak in bullets, have something to say, do not ramble
- ☐ Listen actively
- ☐ Be supportive—praise peers
- ☐ Be inclusive—spread the credit
- ☐ Disagreements—principle-based, not people-based

TEAM TOOL #5

Productively Managing Team Conflict

One of the most difficult leadership skills to develop is that of productively managing conflict. Being productive means having the strength to keep your eyes on the vision and making decisions that support the vision. Sometimes those decisions are not the most popular, which will create conflict. Often, team members will lose sight of the vision and intra-team conflict will occur. How the team leader deals with team conflict can be a distinguishing factor in the success of the team.

There are three things a team leader should know when dealing with team conflict. First, the leader needs to recognize conflict and how it manifests itself in the team system. Second, there needs to be an understanding of why conflict occurs in the team. Finally, insights into and techniques on managing conflict will be presented in this chapter.

What Is Conflict and How Does It Manifest Itself in the Team?

We know what conflict is because it often comes with a "feeling"—a feeling of contempt, anger, negativity, hostility, jealousy or many other destructive emotions. What we need to focus on as team leaders is a constructive way of viewing conflict.

According to the book *Tools for Teams*, there are two kinds of conflict:

1. Emotional conflict is referred to as A-Type conflict and is personally destructive.

2. Cognitive conflict is referred to as C-Type conflict which is depersonalized and focuses on problem solutions. C-Type conflict drives creative problem solving and innovation.

A-Type conflict will cause counterproductive behavior and distractions from the goal or vision. It will destroy task focus and drain the energy from the team. It is a team leader's challenge to convert A-Type conflict to the more productive C-Type conflict as soon as possible.

In the publication *Group Decision and Negotiation*, Shah and Jehn discovered that C-Type conflict is more prevalent in teams where the members have a foundation of friendship. New teams or teams of strangers showed a much less sophisticated conflict management process and were less task-productive.

It is the team leader's responsibility to sense conflict. A leader's intuition and gut feeling should be sharp enough to see potential problems. Reciprocity is usually framed in a positive way: Do good things for others and they will pass the goodwill on. Negative reciprocity is the compounding or expectation of negative results. Some of the ways that negative reciprocity is seen in the workplace can be the catalyst for conflict.

- Hoarding resources
- Returning insults
- Ignoring an indifferent worker
- Making rude gestures
- Gossiping
- Purposely doing work incorrectly
- Getting people back

(Partial list from *How to Reduce Workplace Conflict and Stress* by A. Maravelas)

Some of the warning signs that should trigger a leader's intuition would include any of the following situations:

- If someone on the team assumes that a task is being handled or that a person is responsible for something that has not been confirmed. Being in a lead position, you may hear of these expectations.

- A team member's ulterior motive or personal agenda has redirected the reason for completing a task. Keep the team focused on the real team vision.

- Misunderstandings, misinterpretations and assumptions can create conflict when there is a lack of communication. Teach the team the art of clarifying and create an environment open to clarification.

- One team member has become overly dependent on another team member. This situation can cause inefficiency and animosity and rob the team leaders of a training opportunity.

- If there is a need for consensus on an outcome, there will be a greater possibility for conflict. The leader may need to negotiate the outcome to ensure all parties' involvement.

- As rules, policies and expectations are defined, any enforcement of the rules may cause conflict among those that disagree. The key to addressing this warning sign is consistency. Treating every team member the same sets the understanding of equal consequences.

Conflict can manifest itself in many ways and for many reasons. Listening to the gut feeling that conflict may be brewing does not mean that a punitive or punishment-based approach needs to be taken. A corrective approach with a sense of concern will go a long way in addressing an issue. This corrective approach is focused on correcting the problem to make the team as productive as they can be. Any behavioral correction should maintain the productivity purpose.

There are four basic reasons why conflict occurs within a team, and there are just as many good ways to address the *problem* instead of the emotions behind it:

1. A difference in facts or data has been discovered. The basis for resolving this potential conflict is to go to the source. Facts and data are documented. Use the documentation to avert or defuse any A-Type conflict that may arise.

2. The process or methods of achieving a goal have been challenged with an alternative approach. To resolve a conflict based on this difference of opinion, there must be productive discussion. This is where C-Type conflict can really be beneficial. Focus on the problem and not the people to make a decision best suited for the final goal.

3. If the purpose or goal of the project or team is not clear, there is an increased potential for conflict throughout the life of the team. Resolution for this source of conflict must include the team leader and any management involved in supporting the team. If the team leader has established a solid foundation (see *Team Tool #4*) which includes a team vision, the team will be clear on its purpose. If the confusion persists, the discussion and ultimate resolution will be the team leader's decision.

4. Value differences are direct results of our life experiences and our personal commitments. It takes a significant emotional event to change a value belief. If a personal value difference is the source of a conflict, then the leader should focus the team on the common ground they all share—and that is the team vision. If the value difference is a professional one, then the member with the differing opinion may need to leave the team. A personal value difference might be one on abortion, politics or religion. A professional value difference may be one on financial reporting or ethics. In either case, the member must make a decision about whether the value difference directly affects their ability to achieve the team goal.

A-Type conflict is fueled by emotion—usually because of one of the previously mentioned sources. Thoughts drive our emotions, and our emotions drive our actions. Here is an example of how that might flow for the following conflict sources:

Conflict Situation	Possible Thoughts	Various Emotions
An argument breaks out about the use of a non-approved vendor.	1. "I don't have to follow the rules." 2. "This is a better vendor." 3. "I told this vendor I would buy from them." 4. "My friend works for this vendor."	1. Arrogance 2. Overconfidence 3. Embarrassment 4. Loyalty
Two members disagree on how a piece of equipment is to be installed.	1. "This person doesn't know what he's talking about." 2. "We've never done it that way." 3. "This person is new to the team." or "This person is only 20 years old." 4. "I've done this a million times."	1. Mistrust 2. Fear 3. Lack of respect 4. Pride
There is a difference of opinion on the purpose of a volunteer team—to raise money or to raise awareness.	1. "I don't know how to do that." 2. "I don't want to do that." 3. "I don't have time to do that." 4. "It's not our job to do that."	1. Embarrassment 2. Fear of others' opinions 3. Fear of losing control, not knowing how to say "No." 4. Fear of conflict
Two workers have a difference of opinion about politics, and it's keeping them from working together.	1. "I've done more research." 2. "I form my own opinions." 3. "I have personal experience and they don't."	1. Misplaced self-confidence 2. Arrogance 3. Pride

How to Manage Team Conflict

Once a foundation of conflict acceptance is in place, the leader is ready to teach the team how to deal with conflict issues.

Team communication is at its best when ideas are shared, suggestions are taken and discussed, support is given and conflict is creative and collaborative. You can feel the electric energy in the room. On the other hand, when one person dominates a conversation, ideas are rejected and the team is locked in nonproductive circular discussions, conflict rules the team and meetings are frustrating. As the team leader, there are three skill areas you can use to guide your team and prepare them for successful team challenges:

1. **Foundation:** Create a safe foundation for addressing team conflict

   Team members need to feel that they can disagree within the team and not be subject to team rejection or retaliation. Two documents established in *Team Tool #4 – Laying the Foundation for a Productive Team* are essential for the team to create a safe place for discussions about conflict issues. The Team Charter will contain the team vision, and the Rules of Engagement for Meetings will establish the behavior boundaries for meeting etiquette. One of the best things the leader can do for the team is build the relationships between team members by giving them the opportunities to get to know each other outside of the office. Allow them to take off their work mask and put on their fun mask. Some individuals are more protective at work than others. Familiarization will contribute to a safe foundation.

2. **Facilitation:** Create a facilitation process for addressing team conflict

   There are three parts to establishing a facilitation process for the team. They must know how to start the conversation, effectively listen and productively solve conflict.

   Teach them how to start conflict discussions:

   - Decide if the issue should be addressed with the individual or brought to the team. This assessment can be made based on the project magnitude or the issue of conflict and if it involves one individual or a group.

   - Teach your team the value of controlling their emotions when discussing confrontational issues. The best way to teach is to model the behavior you want.

   - Help them to use self-disclosing language. *Team Tool #3* taught the leader to use "I" statements, which will keep the tone of a discussion focused on the speaker's experience, and not using an accusatory "you." Share your knowledge.

   - Teach them how to be inclusive. Look at the team picture and consider that there might be many contributing factors and many potential resolutions.

Teach them how to Power Listen. The book *Crucial Conversations* cites three keys to Power Listening.

- *Be sincere.* This means to make comfortable eye contact and be mentally present when listening.
- *Be curious.* Ask questions; clarify your understanding of the speaker.
- *Be patient.* Let the speaker complete their sentences and do not interrupt.

Two of the biggest challenges for any listener are focus and control. Distractions— environmental, personal or mental—can break a listener's attention and contribute to the conflict. Responsive emotions can be controlled through reflective statements when responding or clarifying. A reflective statement is one that reflects feelings, facts or understanding. If a speaker is passionate about a topic, reflect the feelings heard in the speaker's voice: "I can tell this is very important to you." Reflect the facts or your understanding if the tone of the speaker elicits a confrontational emotion.

Support the team in its solution challenges. The team leader is in a position to resolve priority issues if there are competing tasks. This is an excellent time to re-emphasize focus on the team goal or vision as the driving force. The team leader is also in a position to bridge any ability gaps that may be affecting the goal completion. This provides an opportunity to cross-train and expand the skills of your team members. If skill development is preempted by time constraints, the long-term development of the team members will suffer.

3. **Fortification.** Create a personal fortification system to support your team members.

   Dealing with criticism is a difficult personal challenge. During conflict discussions, nonperformance may be discussed, and without personal fortitude, performance discussions might be mistaken as rejection of the team member. Here are four tips to share with your team to support their personal strength during a conflict discussion.

   - Understand that we perceive ourselves as vulnerable when criticized. This can cause defensiveness.
   - The comfort of the team and the environment will improve receptivity
   - Emphasize personal improvement or goal achievement instead of blame
   - Show concern for all team members because you never know when your report, your decision or your actions might be the source of a future issue

Top 10 Tough Tips

Finally, here are 10 tried and true tactics that will help you fortify the strength of your team's communication:

1. Don't keep revisiting team issues—your meetings will start to resemble the movie *Groundhog Day*!

2. Assure the team that it is OK to confront an authority figure, probably the team leader, if that leader could be part of the problem

3. Reassure the team that bringing a nonstandard approach to the table could be the grounds for C-Type conflict and be very creative for the team

4. Teach the team that a silent person can rob the team of viable ideas, slow the team down and be counterproductive

5. Don't use hearsay as support for an action

6. Deal with devastating news in as timely, honest and factual a manner as you can

7. Do not allow threats in the team environment

8. Don't encourage the team to change their work process when it is not supported by the behavior of other employees

9. Turn down projects based on specifics such as time and resources, and it will be accepted by the team

10. Instill the team belief that changes in behavior and positive results are possible

Recognizing conflict, understanding why it occurs and knowing how to effectively address the problems will be the keys to proving leadership skills. To learn and share these skills not only will insure a better working relationship within the team but also will have a positive influence on the company culture.

TEAM TOOL #6

Keeping the Team Fired Up

In the previous chapter we learned how to deal with conflict. In some cases, when conflict is addressed, it leaves a void for those that were so used to it. Giving your team credit for their accomplishments can fill that void. The importance of motivating the team is more than filling a void; it has long-reaching benefits for the leader as well as the team member. Being able to encourage others to perform is a skill and is one of the most enviable talents a leader can acquire. This chapter will cover the basic understanding of what it takes to support the performance of a team so they continue to be fired up about their tasks, their team and their company.

For a team leader, motivation is the art of influence. For a team member, motivation is the will to act. It is the leader's challenge to influence team members to act for the goal or vision of the group. Having some fun along the way keeps the team coming back.

Motivation goes to the heart of each individual team member, so know your team to make sure your choice of motivation technique or tactic is compatible. Consider four basic positive reinforcement actions:

1. **Verbal/social:** Praise given either in verbal, written, direct or indirect form is the best example of verbal/social positive reinforcement. When praise is given to a team member, it should be public, prompt and delivered in a purposeful manner. Know whether your team member appreciates public recognition and act accordingly.

2. **Tangible/symbolic:** Achievement awards, special parking places, Employee of the Month and The Million Dollar Club are all tangible and give the recipient a certain status.

3. **Work-related:** This recognition includes promotions, special assignments, special training—anything that is directly related to furthering the team member's career.

4. **Financial:** This cost-based positive reinforcement should be used with caution. It includes bonuses, raises, profit sharing, stock options and other monetary items. Often these become a substitute for the personal touch. They become expected with no correlation to the quality of work performed. When this happens, the reward system becomes a transaction-oriented program and loses its value as a positive reinforcement.

Any program that you put in place should address one of the eight core human desires. These are the drivers for the human will to act.

Does your motivating action or team member recognition:

1. Credit an action?

2. Create the feeling of ownership?

3. Give power?

4. Support affiliation?

5. Enhance competence?

6. Celebrate achievement?

7. Give recognition?

8. Have meaning?

At least one of these drivers will go to the heart of each team member, and that fuels the will for each one to continue performing at the level that you are recognizing.

Team leaders know when their team members are in the "zone of achievement" because the job done well becomes the fuel that drives continued results. Because not all members are in the "zone," there will be a need to measure just how motivated your team members are.

There are seven factors that indicate the level of motivation in the workplace:

1. How much work is being completed?

2. How much effort does it take to do the work?

3. Is the team focused on their tasks?

4. Do people enjoy working together?

5. Are intentions of the members goal focused?

6. Is overachievement the tone of the team?

7. Do the team members volunteer to help each other?

The answers to these questions will help the team leader gauge the result of or the need for motivation within the team. As the team is evaluated, also consider any unintentional contributions you may be making to undermine the motivation efforts. Here is a self-assessment list:

- Have you created the right work environment to accept your motivation efforts?

- Do you know the basic human needs for clear expectations, opportunities and the desire to get along?

- Have you controlled the Big Three factors?

  1. Created stability
  2. Taken action when needed
  3. Secured the future of the team

- Do you avoid the seven self-defeating sins?

  1. Needing to be liked vs. respected
  2. Depending on the team's advice
  3. Sticking to the rules at the expense of team talents
  4. Criticizing in a nonconstructive manner
  5. Not keeping the team responsible
  6. Not treating all team members the same
  7. Failing to keep the team informed

How to Motivate a Team

The Three Levels of Team Motivation That the Leader Can Create

1. Team identity motivation

Creating a team identity is an important part of giving the team a cohesive feeling of purpose. Here are several ideas that might bring the group together and create the same feeling of camaraderie as one might have for their favorite sports team:

- **Team name:** Let the team choose a name. It can be based on their purpose, their talents, their project or whatever brought them together

- **Team mascot:** A live mascot is usually out of the question, but a stuffed animal or a picture would work

- **Team song:** Have the team pick a song that gets the group fired up and play it at the team meetings and any special team recognition events

- **Team colors:** Your favorite sports team has colors, so can your team. Wear them, display them and let everyone know what they represent.

- **Team logo:** Let the team design or pick a logo from the Internet. Use it in signature lines; have it put on t-shirts, coffee cups, pens, pencils or group documentation. It is often best to include the company logo alongside the team logo to emphasize the affiliation.

- **Team motto:** This slogan should be publicized everywhere in the team work area. Screen savers, e-mail signatures and wall hangings should display the team motto

- **Team star:** Have the team name assigned to a star (www.starregistry.com) and post the star chart in the team area

2. Leader-to-team motivation

The second level of team motivation is between the leader and the team. It is the team leader's responsibility to initiate a motivational program for their team. You don't need to spend a lot of money to show your team that you appreciate them and to encourage them to continue doing a great job.

The easiest way to get ideas on how your team would like to be rewarded is to ask them. Having a brainstorming session on this topic can be fun and motivating by itself. Keep in mind that when you do something fun for your team, connect it to a team achievement; otherwise, the team may begin to expect the rewards without the hard work.

Here are some ideas for motivating your team:

- **Car wash:** Challenge the team to meet a deadline. Once completed, collect your team in the parking lot on a Friday afternoon and let the team members sit on the sidelines drinking lemonade, while the managers, team leaders and supervisors wash the team members' cars.

- **Movie break:** After a milestone is met, let the team take a long lunch and either go to a movie or cater lunch in and show a movie in the conference room

- **Ice cream sundaes:** Let the team take an afternoon break and bring in ice cream and everything to make sundaes to congratulate them on meeting a deadline

- **Voice mail thanks:** Send out a funny voice mail to each of your team members thanking them for all of their effort

- **Thank-you cards:** Send a handwritten thank-you card to each member at their home to thank them for their hard work. Have the next level of management also sign the card.

- **"Secret Agent":** If your team members have to travel away from their families and they have children, send a note to their children telling them their parent is on a "secret mission" for the company. Put in a fast food gift card for them. If the employee is single, send them a thank you note with a restaurant or movie gift card.

- **Pat on the back:** Make a copy of your hand on the copy machine and write a note of thanks on the bottom and tape it to each team member's door or chair so everyone can see it

- **Team Appreciation Day:** If you have a talent like cooking, gardening, writing or baking, bring something you have made for your team members or buy something for them. Make it a big deal.

3. Intra-team motivation

The third level of team motivation is connecting the team members to each other. Building a working relationship between team members is the foundation of trust and will reduce conflict and increase productivity. The best way to connect your team is to get them outside of the office. Here are some activities you can put into action to begin helping your team members get to know and relate to each other:

- Start a sports team and enter into a community intramural league—let the team pick which sport and have jobs for those that cannot play the sport
- Take the team to a sports event—baseball, football, hockey or basketball. Pick up the cost of hot dogs or have a tailgate party.
- Take them bowling
- Set up a deep-sea fishing excursion. If everyone can't go, invite them over for fish after the trip.
- Take them to play miniature golf
- Have a competition on who can build the best miniature golf hole in their office
- Have each team member build something out of Legos
- Plan a happy hour escape—take them out of the office in the middle of the day for coffee or milk shakes
- Set up a "Gotcha" program that allows team members to nominate their peers for doing something right or for contributing to the team in an extraordinary way. Once nominated, the recipient will get a gift card, coupon for the company store, a $5 bill or some token of recognition and appreciation.

The bottom-line benefits to keeping your team fired up lie in your two ultimate leader goals:

1. Create a high-performing team
2. Develop each team member to their fullest capability

When you support them, they will grow. When they grow, so will your leadership credibility.

TEAM TOOL #7

Keeping the Team On Track

Motivation is not the same as momentum, but it does play an important role in creating momentum for achieving results and fueling progress. This chapter will tell you how to create the momentum to get and keep your team on track. The leader will need to learn how to keep the team members focused, remove process barriers and support and celebrate their performance. Creating momentum is just like running around a track— The Performance Track.

The Performance Track

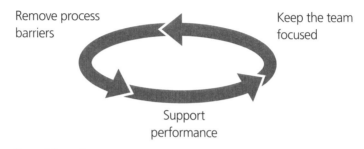

Remove process barriers

Keep the team focused

Support performance

Thomas Wilson identified six principles to follow in keeping your team on track in his book *Innovative Reward Systems for the Changing Workplace*:

1. Keep the team focused on who the real recipient of their work is. Knowing that the job they do ultimately affects an individual can create a level of commitment that will fuel performance.

2. Break down any walls, real or perceived, that may be interfering with getting the team's tasks done on time. These barriers could be resources, people or business processes.

3. Help the team maximize their effectiveness. One-on-one time with each team member will promote brainstorming of personal efficiency ideas for that individual. This time together will also help to build the relationship between you and your team that is needed throughout The Performance Track.

4. Through any learning curve the team member may have, include lots of positive feedback for positive results. This feedback will fuel more work and increase the speed of positive results.

5. Help them to realize that continual improvement is part of the momentum that will make them successful. Without an open mind for change, enhanced performance opportunities may be missed.

6. Support their performance. Team results are required, there is no option for failing to meet the goal, but appreciation from the leader goes a long way toward refueling the engine for the next trip around The Performance Track.

Here is a checklist of barriers you may run into and some thoughts to promote solutions:

- ☐ Do you know the key decision makers in organizational service areas that the team uses? (You may need to move fast to solve a problem and these contacts could help.)

- ☐ Have you gotten buy-in from the customer on a project approach? (Customer involvement at key points can avoid re-work.)

- ☐ Are all expectations—yours, the team's and the client's—on the table? (Your expectations must be understood so that you are not contributing to the team barriers.)

- ☐ Do you have a process for dealing with conflict? (Follow *Team Tool #3* to build your personal communication methods and follow *Team Tools #4* and *#5* to teach the team how to manage conflict.)

- ☐ Does the team bring all issues to the table and keep no surprises? (Is the team receptive and open to discussion of issues?)

- ☐ Do you know how to keep the work flowing, even during times of challenge? (Do you keep them learning?)

- ☐ Is everyone receiving the same level of support from you? (Don't let your window of perception affect the performance of the team.)

The obstacles that a leader has direct control over are those that leadership skills are built around. If there is a solid vision for the team, there will be a strong sense of direction. If conflict and issues are addressed immediately, the team will not see conflict as an issue. If a team charter has been established with member expectations detailed, there will be no question about taking responsibility and paying the consequences for not following through. If the leader has spent the time to establish a solid business relationship with each team member, there will be no question about trust. If the leader has the best interest of the team members at heart, the skill gaps will be seen and addressed. If the leader has focused on building the member relationships, obstacles will be few and easy to address.

Supporting Performance

Keeping the team focused on the vision and clearing the way for them to be successful will build task completion appeal. As performance increases, satisfaction increases and the little things like shortcomings and mistakes are dealt with constructively instead of destructively. The final stretch of The Performance Track requires two things: collaboration and commitment.

Collaboration is the key to performance. Without it, the group would not be, by definition, a team. Your work as the team leader has molded the group into a team. The team has fostered positive interdependence through the relationships that have been established and the shared support between members. Once the expectation of collaboration and performance is set and followed, there is a high level of competence that a team reaches which is considered the most effective stage of team development, the performing stage. At this level, not only has the team reached peak performance but your leadership skills are now recognized by your peers and the company.

There are five self-evaluation questions you can use to judge your own level of team leadership skill development:

1. Can you quantify your team's progress?

2. Is your team making fact-based decisions, having a customer focus and supporting each others' ideas?

3. Have you developed your team members and created a learning culture?

4. Is there an equal balance of work among the team?

5. Does the team self-check and have a performance-minded culture?

Answering these questions will help you assess how far you have come in building your leadership skills. Just as you are committed to becoming the best leader you can be, you also are modeling for the team what it takes to fulfill a commitment. The team must see the clarity of purpose you have and feel the level of trust you have placed in them.

Commitment can be undermined when the team feels a need for consensus and absolute certainty. This avoidance of risk can foster a level of mistrust between individuals and create an unsure atmosphere between members. Without commitment, there is ambiguity, excessive analysis, lack of confidence, fear of failure and a nonproductive environment. Second-guessing is encouraged, and decisions are revisited often.

Commitment requires taking a risk for the larger vision instead of focusing on the closer or short-term task. Risk becomes part of the adrenaline rush of a high-performance team.

To tie all of this together, good teams will have a leader that lends clarity to the group, promotes the common goals, ensures a learning environment, helps the members seize opportunities to move forward and teaches collaboration and commitment. There are two benefits of effective team leadership:

1. Personal achievement of building leadership skills

2. Personal satisfaction of building a high-performance team

As the team moves around The Performance Track they will benefit from:

- Increased productivity
- Enhanced reward opportunities
- Future learning
- A set foundation for growth
- Skill increase

TEAM TOOL #8

Keeping the Team Accountable

> "People hold inside themselves the power to rise above their circumstances and get the results they want."
>
> *– The Oz Principle*

Holding a team accountable conjures up different images for different people. In the business world, it means helping others be responsible for results that ultimately make them a success. Successful leaders see accountability as a key to their team's success. This tool will look at accountability from the leader's view and the team member's view. You will learn how to guide your team to results without using forceful compliance or fault-finding.

What Is Accountability and Why Do We Need It?

Team accountability is the willingness of peers to make suggestions on performance improvement behaviors that affect the team. Within the team, members must feel comfortable giving and receiving suggestions. This is difficult for most teams in the early stages because members are neither accustomed to nor are they willing to tolerate their personal discomfort to mention to a peer that their behavior is not productive. And of course, there is the general tendency to avoid conflict. As the team leader, the responsibility is to set a professional tone for team interaction and redirect any emotionally based comments. At the same time, the leader must be willing to allow the team to self-correct, trust team members' judgment and be willing to serve as the ultimate arbitrator of discipline if needed.

Team members should be held accountable to not just the expected team results but also to the process expectations. These expectations have been specified in the Team Charter and the Rules of Engagement for Meetings as guided in *Team Tool #4*. These documents make the team leader's job of accountability much easier. There is an additional facet to accountability the leader is responsible for. Can you answer these questions positively and confidently?

- Did you grow the enterprise?
- Did the enterprise achieve a level of prominence?
- Did you leave a legacy?

The leader's performance against these measures is the "final frontier" of accountability for a successful leader.

If results are not measured and tracked, the team will lose sight of the value of productivity, and four behaviors will begin to take over:

1. Resentment will begin to grow over small issues

2. Mediocrity will become the accepted performance level

3. Deadlines and key deliverables will be missed

4. The team will not be empowered to self-correct, and the team leader will become the sole source of discipline

On the other hand, if accountability is fostered and supported, there will be four more productive behaviors exhibited:

1. Team members will ensure that poor performers improve, thus helping the leader build the skill level of the staff

2. Problems will be addressed and resolved more quickly

3. The team will value and respect the level of standards that have been put in place

4. The team's self-correction ultimately will reduce the bureaucracy surrounding the organization's performance management process

Measuring the team's performance will give the leader a continued opportunity to catch the members doing something right—at which point direct positive reinforcement is appropriate. Searching for a personal support behavior is the extra push needed to get a team member around The Performance Track described in *Team Tool #7*.

There are two measurements that the team and the leader are held accountable for: results and behavior. Results are the measure of performance, the amount of output, the quantifiable impact on the organization. Behavioral measurement is tracking the method or process used to get the result. Each of these measurements is used at different times and in different situations. Two examples from Aubrey and James Daniels' book *Measure of a Leader* include:

1. Hold the team strictly accountable to results when:

   • Current results are good and only small improvements are needed

   • Results are improving and you need to reinforce progress

   • Team members are highly skilled and increasing the result will be a positive challenge

   • There is a tight correlation between behavior and result. In this case, the group has a direct visible control of their productivity.

2. Hold the team accountable to the behavior or process standards when:

- Performance of the team is a long way from the intended goal

- New skills are needed

- There is a long interval between the behavior and the visible result

- There are many outside variables and forces affecting the result and it is hard to isolate the team's specific contribution

With these standards, the team leader has a platform on which accountability can be built. Do you have these measurable standards in place?

- Vision/Mission Statement

- Team Charter

- Rules of Engagement for Meetings

- Job descriptions

- Performance standards

- Organizational policies

Each of these contributes to the success of the team and to the success of your leadership credibility.

In *Team Tool #7* we discussed keeping the team focused. When it comes to focusing on accountability for results, the customer will play a major role in determining if the result is acceptable. The team needs to know who their customers are. Customers can be internal to the organization or external and are just as important as the team vision to hone the team's attention. Their requirements and expectations must be well publicized within the team. Consider compiling a Customer Focus Form that would include information such as:

- A customer profile

- Key success factors

- Performance requirements

- Behavioral requirements

The Customer Focus Form could be compiled in the following manner, depending on who your customers are:

- **Internal teams** (office staff, accounting departments, technology support teams) would interview a sampling of the various departments, management levels or offices they serve. Each team member could do one interview, fill out a Customer Focus Form, then post the forms in a common work area.

- **Sales teams** (both internal and external sales) would use one form per customer to build understanding and rapport. These customer discussions will leave no expectations unrealized or assumptions to question.

Discovering the foundation for keeping your team responsible is easy; helping them maintain a high level of accountability is not as easy. There are several things you can do to keep them on top. First, be very alert to any signs of the team slipping into the victim cycle.

One of the best books on accountability in the workplace was written by Roger Connors, Tom Smith and Craig Hickman and is called *The Oz Principle*. Their approach to defining accountability was based on the characters from *The Wizard of Oz* and how each character lacked a key factor of being responsible for their own results. Connor, Smith and Hickman cite six sources of unaccountability that they say is Below the Line® behavior.

1. Team members will ignore or deny a task

2. Team members will declare the task is not their job

3. A team member will blame someone else

4. The team member will do only what they are told

5. The member will do things to cover incorrect behavior, actions or decisions

6. A team member will do nothing and wait to see if someone notices the mistake

These unacceptable behaviors can appear on any team and need to be addressed immediately using the same awareness/concern approach we learned in *Team Tool #5 – Productively Managing Team Conflict*. Remove these issues from the team's path of productivity.

Team members are not the only contributors to Below the Line® behavior. There are two areas where leaders unintentionally contribute to the unaccountability of their team, individually and collectively. From an individual standpoint, each team member is evaluated on whether they are performing. Sometimes a leader measures on a differing scale due to a multitude of different biases that have been studied. Following is a list of common biases that send a mixed message on what performance is required to give the expected results:

- **Leniency bias:** The leader accepts substandard performance. This is also known as pampering or over-evaluating a team member's performance. It ultimately will affect all other systems (compensation, promotion, training and development).

- **Under-evaluating:** The leader does not give credit where credit is due. This robs the leader of a valuable opportunity to promote acceptable performance and sends a demotivating message to the rest of the team.

- **Double standard:** The leader is not using the same level of expectations for the team member, including the leader. It is the leader's responsibility to lead by example and follow the same expectations for results.

- **The halo effect:** The leader has placed more emphasis on the performance of one team member to the exclusion of others.

- **The horn error:** The leader has a noticeable bias against a team member for reasons that may have nothing to do with performance on the team.

Another collective contribution that managers need to be aware of is making sure that resources are available so the team can meet its expected results. Resources also include having the proper training and a stable work environment. Holding yourself accountable to recognizing your contributions, seeing what action you can take, owning the expected result, resolving the victim mentality and finally taking action will provide the team with a great model to follow.

The measurement of performance directly impacts future behavior, so the achievement of goals, the accomplishment of tasks and the delivery of results need to be publicly recognized. Publish and post all completions. Regularly review the progress against expectations and celebrate with team rewards. Neglecting to support your team in this manner will be one of those contributing factors to the decline of team performance.

PART 3

Public Skills for Team Recognition

TEAM TOOL #9

Advertising the Team's Success

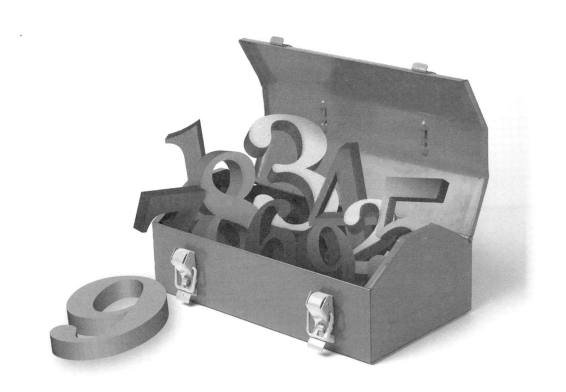

Leadership is putting your team in front and giving them the credit.

This chapter addresses an often overlooked but critical step in team leadership—advertising your team's success. Our focus has been on the team, building relationships, increasing productivity and keeping the team motivated. Advertising is the next logical step because giving credit for doing a great job is only a part of the team reward system.

Advertising is broader and deeper than just giving the team credit and can be understood best by exploring the answers to four key questions:

1. Why advertise?

2. Advertise what?

3. Who needs to know?

4. How can you effectively get this done?

Why Advertise?

Why worry about advertising at all? Some might say that advertising is simply a motivational tool. The purpose for advertising is not to motivate the team but to motivate everyone else: management, the company, the customers, the vendors and the community. Advertising will expand public awareness of the team's accomplishments, and two things will occur:

1. Response to the advertising will provide additional support to lift up team members

2. Others will see the importance of this critical step in team success

The team's accomplishments will bring additional opportunities to the leader and the team members. Advertising increases exposure of the team's purpose within the company and increases department visibility. Putting the team first and the leader second is not easy for everyone. The team leader must have a servant leadership mentality to accomplish this. If the team comes first, their needs and their accomplishments come first. Your actions become an example to other leaders as a road map for success.

Another reason to advertise success is to capitalize on the motivation that it infuses into the team environment. The attention alone will be enough to revitalize a mentally and physically exhausted team. This added attention will promote team member talents and make them and their skills recognizable.

The ultimate purpose of advertising is to promote the project results. Advertising is a critical step that will inspire the team and enhance the leader's personal value, but company results should remain the focus of the advertising purpose. The results of the project, department or cross-functional team must bring value to the company in a definable way that advances either performance or market share.

Advertise What?

Project results have been measured as the team has progressed to the goal. These measurements represent change. These changes must be quantified in order to be valued. These quantifiable results are the foundation of the material to be advertised.

Quantification of results should be linked to the company vision, department purpose and team charter in a form that can be understood. There are two general foundations for results that can be advertised:

1. **Economic-based.** Economic results are related to the consumption or utilization of company resources.

2. **Value-based.** Value results pertain to behaviors or relationships established by the team for the organization.

The table below gives several examples of economic-based and value-based results. Refer to *Team Tool #8* for additional support on putting these measures in place and holding the team accountable to them.

Economic-based measurements	Value-based measurements
Increased production	Customer satisfaction
Reduction of waste	Added skill/service ability
Reduced time	Risk reduction
Reduced cost	New process introduction
Increased access	Reliability
Accuracy	Service
Re-work reduction	Market position
Customer returns	Time to market

When the team brings about a change in an organization, there will be two important components:

1. The change will have features, such as a new piece of equipment or a new process

2. The change will have benefits, such as increased production or improved customer satisfaction. It is the change benefits that need to be advertised, and that will produce the support you need to promote your team.

Advertise to Whom?

Who is the best target audience to hear about the team accomplishments? There are seven different audiences that can maximize the promotion payoff:

1. **Other internal departments within the organization.** To get the full internal organizational benefit from the team's results, other departments must be aware of what is available for them to use. Whether it's economic- or value-based, other departments can either utilize the change or model your process for achieving the change.

2. **Other locations within the same organization.** Communication between remote locations within an organization is often poor. The effect of advertising results between locations will maximize the benefits that the team can bring to an organization. Other locations may be able to use the results directly or other locations' management may utilize the model to promote change within their locations.

3. **Deeper and higher organization management.** Management awareness of the results will accomplish several things. Positive awareness will spread the word of success as well as become a jumping-off point for enhancement of the results produced. The level of achieved results may become the expected productivity norm of any team.

4. **Customers.** Advertising to customers can be the ultimate organizational benefit the team could provide. Customer relations are the life blood of any organization. Direct positive influence on those relationships will increase the tools available to promote your team.

5. **Vendors.** Vendors are more difficult to use as an advertising medium. If a project or team has been the first to utilize a vendor's product or method, it is best to partner with the vendor to guarantee the success of that purchase and become a testimonial for them. This relationship expands the reach of awareness to a market that may otherwise not be accessible. There are times when the specific use of a vendor's product or service is part of a company's secrets and should not be revealed. For the most part, when vendors become partners in the result, they will become more oriented to serving the team's continued needs.

6. **The community.** Community awareness of an organization's projects and team results goes directly to organizational value. No matter what your organization does, a solid public image is a competitive edge.

7. **Global contacts.** To advertise results globally could be done through an organization's global presence, or it could apply to just getting the word out worldwide for a local organization. Internet marketing is the simplest way to accomplish this level of promotion.

Any time results are advertised, results are enhanced. Whether economic- or value-based, to tell people of a change that has been effective will support or promote a comfort level with change. For this reason, when the achievements are promoted, there must be a link to the organization's purpose.

How to Advertise

Since advertising is a critical step in the ongoing success of the team, all forms of advertising should be considered. There are four general media to be considered: paper, electronic, audio and video. The word-of-mouth method of promotion is covered separately. Let's take a look at what can be done.

Paper	Electronic	Audio	Video
Charts and graphs	Intranet	Voice mail	On any Web site
Project plans	Company Web site	Audio file on any Web site	DVD production
Top Five reports	Team Web site	CD production	Video shown at executive meeting
Newsletters	Blog	MP3 file	Video set up in the lobby for visitors to see
Annual Reports	E-mail	Podcast	
Special announcements		Radio promotion	
Local newspapers			
Trade magazines			
Press releases			

Paper

The paper medium is good to create visual promotion in a local environment, but it loses its cost effectiveness to the electronic medium when the audience goes beyond the local group. Charts, graphs and project plans can be posted outside the department or team area to show progress. Continual visual reinforcement has great value not only for the organization to see the results but also as a motivator for the team. The Top Five Report is a regular report that targets only five key items for a specified period of time such as a month. These items are described in measurable terms and directly related to the team, departmental or organizational purpose. If the organization already has a paper-based newsletter, write an article, be a guest columnist or set up an ongoing column that publicizes team accomplishments. If the team leader cannot write a column, then delegate or circulate the responsibility. Newspapers and magazines always are looking for articles. This exposure will not only advertise the team but also promote the organization to the world through the publication's distribution channel.

Electronic

Electronic methods of communication are more convenient and cost-effective today. Organizational intranets often have departmental Web pages that are a great source for team exposure. The organization's public Web site would be a great place for a press release or project completion announcement. It is very easy to set up a separate Web site for the team as a means of team communication and team recognition. Include a blog and encourage team members to post their ideas or comments.

Audio

Audio promotion can be as simple as an organization voice mail announcement or as complex as a promotional radio program. A short audio file can be attached to any Web site, sent as a part of an e-mail or turned into an MP3 or podcast file.

Video

If professionally done, video can be the most costly and complex of the promotional options, but if handled in an informal manner, it could be a great team escape. With the proliferation and popularity of "reality shows" on television, casual video is more accepted. To collect accounts of celebrations and challenges along the way gives the team visual footage to document their success. A documentary could be put together and presented at an executive meeting or an all-employee meeting or played in the lobby for visitors and customers to see.

Word of mouth

The most time-consuming method of advertising is word of mouth because it involves multiple presentations or one-on-one discussions. The presentations would not necessarily be just to the organization. If the project results are of interest to the community, it may involve interviews with or presentations to local service organizations or trade associations.

Not all of these options are suitable for all project, organization or team accomplishments. Some teams carry more responsibility for strategic organizational change and would require more intense advertising of their achievements. No matter the size of your team, the size of their results or the advertising resources you have available to you, this critical step should be a part of your team leader toolkit. Ultimately the leader is responsible for performance of the team and making sure the team results meet organizational expectations. Advertising doesn't just happen; the leader must:

- Design the program

- Plan the promotion and budget

- Implement the plan

- Manage the result

Get the team involved. Don't forget your marketing and public relations departments, and don't try to do this all yourself.

TEAM TOOL #10

Fulfilling Each Team Member's Vision of Success

> "It takes a leader to raise a leader."

> – John Maxwell

The final tool in the successful team leader's toolkit will help you complete the circle of success for the team. After all, team members have pursued the team vision and have worked hard to overcome conflict in the name of productivity, so it is up to the leader to guarantee that they reap career benefits from their efforts.

We will look at three key factors in achieving this final goal:

1. Creating value for the team member and the team leader

2. The driving force behind fulfilling a dream

3. Completing the circle of success

WIIFM—What's in It for Me, the Team Member?

The important thing for a leader to know is what each team member wants from their career. Not everyone has the same definition of success. Involved team leaders will have learned each individual's career desires and how they can contribute to them.

Based on the Frederick Herzberg employee motivation study from the 1950s, there are four levels of impact that various forms of positive reinforcement have on a team member:

Very High Impact	• Achievement • Recognition
High Impact	• The work itself • Responsibility
Medium Impact	• Advancement • Growth • Salary
Low Impact	• Company policy • Supervision • Relationship with supervisor • Work conditions • Relationship with peers • Personal life • Relationship with subordinates • Status • Security

Herzberg's findings recognize all of the motivators in the workplace and confirm that recognition and a sense of personal achievement have the greatest impact on an individual.

The concept of job enrichment began with Herzberg's study, and the tools in this toolkit have focused on building individual skills that support personal job enrichment. The ultimate in job satisfaction is loving what you do and making a team member's career goals become real to enrich both the member and the leader.

Team members' career goals could include:

- More money
- Qualification for a bonus
- A promotion
- Transfer to a more strategic team
- Increased educational opportunities
- Transfer to another office or area of the country
- The opportunity for international travel or experience
- Additional project responsibility

These goals often are elusive because there has been a paradigm shift in the way employees view their jobs over the last 20 to 30 years. The increase of mergers, acquisitions and bankruptcies has made an indelible mark on the business world. Employees no longer have the same commitment that was once prominent in the workplace. On the other hand, organizations have not shown the loyalty they once had to their workers. Therefore, an employee will define what they need from a company, strive for it, but move on if they cannot get it. Another cultural change that contributes to this shift is that there are more jobs available in the marketplace today. The last two generations have not experienced the job scarcity that the Baby Boomers had in the 1970s. There are more companies, more consumer opportunities, more global opportunities and a change in the workplace model that contributes to the increase in job opportunities. Fulfilling a team member's career goals is now a requirement if you want to retain the knowledge a team member has acquired while serving the team.

As you learn the goals of each team member, document them and follow up regularly to support the achievement process. If the team leader has evaluation responsibility for team members, the documentation of goals will be part of the performance review process. Connect as many tasks and assignments as you can to the achievement of the members' goals so they will realize the continued benefits of performance. Some organizations have a biannual or quarterly process for reviewing performance goals. If your organization does not have such a process, establishing one will help the members keep what's important to them in view. The update meetings do not have to be formal. They are simply to review the team members' achievements and offer any assistance the team leader might provide.

WIIFM—What's in It for Me, the Team Leader?

The team has been developed to benefit not only each team member but also to benefit the company. The human capital asset of the company has increased in value through the team leader's efforts. The company now can be assured there will be competent people to fill new leadership positions that become available. The skills that the team has learned have been centered on fulfilling the company purpose as well as team member goals. The team experience has been fulfilling and challenging to all who have learned from the leader, and key employees have been retained. This strong team leader contribution will increase employee value, reduce employee cost and create long-term potential for growth.

Your efforts as the team leader have been successful, and the following steps should be taken to promote those efforts and the results.

- Create a Team Charter and the Rules of Engagement for Meetings (*Team Tool #4*)
- Establish and follow a conflict management or resolution system (*Team Tool #5*)
- Publicize a Top Five Report of accomplishments on a scheduled basis (*Team Tool #9*)
- Quantify and advertise team achievements (*Team Tools #8 and #9*)

Each of these actions provides documentation of the team leader's results and contributes to proving leadership skills for the team leader's advancement.

To successfully contribute to the team's individual goals, the leader must develop one more skill—that of a mentor. There are three characteristics of a successful mentor:

- Mentors set high expectations
- Mentors are available to their mentees
- Mentors orchestrate developmental experiences

Being a mentor to the team has a two-fold effect. The mentees benefit from the support they receive, and the mentor can relieve some stress. Research has proven that the act of teaching and sharing releases endorphins in our system, thus making mentoring a stress-reducing activity.

John Maxwell defined The Law of Legacy as one of his irrefutable laws of leadership. He states that every leader will leave an organization at some point and each of us should shift our focus to developing leaders instead of leading followers. It is the leader's ultimate responsibility to make the organization as strong as it can be. In building a strong organization through skilled employees, those strong employees will advance and become the leader's legacy.

What Is the Driving Force Behind a Dream?

There are four personal career drivers that support an individual's dream. They include but, as Herzberg observed, are not intended to be in order of importance:

1. Money

2. Status

3. Achievement

4. Recognition

Will everyone respond to these drivers? Probably not. Abraham Maslow's hierarchy of human needs places achievement and recognition close to the top of the hierarchy pyramid. These self-actualization needs are only sought after and fulfilled once the basic personal, safety and familial needs have been met. Discover if there are distractions that are keeping team members from their highest level of achievement and see what you can do to help the team member address the issue to get back to reaching for their career goals (See *Team Tool #5*).

Is everyone cut out to be a leader? Some think that leaders are born. Only 10% of the population has a natural gift for leadership. Another 5% become leaders through a crisis situation, while 85% of the leaders are influenced by another person's leadership skills.

Completing the Circle of Success

There are four final considerations for the leader to complete the circle of personal achievement for a successful team member.

1. **Adaptation of business skills:** Job-related skills should always be maximized within the organization. Ask yourself how a team member's skills can be used in other departments within the company. In *Good to Great*, Jim Collins describes the distinguishing factor between the "Good" organizational leaders and the "Great" organizational leaders as Level Five leadership skills. One of the characteristics of Level Five leadership is the ability to maximize the use of their employee skill base. This ability not only will make the organization stronger but also will bring additional opportunities to team members they might not have considered.

2. **Application of newly acquired team skills:** The dynamics of team relationships are discussed throughout this book. The team has now experienced a structured approach to team success that is not common practice but is a best practice. Allow them to pass these tools on to other teams. As you promote or share your top performers, support them in the application of their newly acquired teambuilding skills.

3. **Association to the organization:** Successful teams get noticed, and through the advertising of the teams' accomplishments, team members will become known to other leaders as high performers. The organization may need those high-performance skills in other locations. Do not be a barrier to the success of your team members by impeding their movement in the organization.

4. **Acceleration of individual careers:** The ultimate in personal satisfaction is to be the catalyst of a great leader's success. Every team member has the potential to be a great leader. It is more important to use the team's success to build a member's career than to build the leader's career. The number of leaders made is the measure of a true leader.

These final considerations are meant to emphasize a servant leader mentality when it comes to building successful leaders. Putting the success of the team members before the success of the leader will guarantee the team members' success and leave the legacy that will guarantee a successful team leader's reputation.

The Toolkit Review

Effective change *always* begins within.

The purpose of this book has been to provide some powerful tools for leadership success. With each tool, the leader has developed skills that will allow them to lead any type of team. The leader has learned the value of teaching teambuilding skills by modeling the behavior for a successful team. To review just how far you have come in building your leadership skills, here is a recap of your new skills and the gifts you gave the team in the process.

Team Tool	The Top 10 Successful Leaders' Team Tools	The Top 10 Lessons for the Team Member
#1	Create a vision for your team to follow and connect everything it does to that vision.	Purpose gives work meaning.
#2	Understand the phases a team goes through and build productive relationships at each phase.	Team phases can be worked through for top performance.
#3	Personal growth of the leader will become a foundation for feedback and effective change.	If the leader can do it, so can I.
#4	Set expectations and abide by them equally and professionally with all.	Team rules are good.
#5	Learn how to address conflict situations through personal control techniques and professional communication.	Conflict isn't so bad when you know what to do.
#6	Motivate the team with events or escapes designed to create momentum.	Work can be productive and fun.
#7	Use "The Performance Track" to keep the team on track with its tasks and projects.	There are others to help me be successful.
#8	Learn the secrets of accountability.	Taking responsibility is connected to team performance.
#9	Advertise their success to those that can best appreciate and promote their individual career goals.	Getting public credit for team accomplishments is motivational.
#10	Be a servant leader by putting the goals of team members first.	My vision of success can be fulfilled through a successful leader.

Your ability to succeed as a team leader is only an action away. You now have the tools to establish solid leadership skills to build a high-performance team.